Jan 18

WHY ARE OSTRICHES SO BIG?

AND OTHER CURIOUS BIRD ADAPTATIONS

BY PATRICIA FLETCHER

Gareth Stevens
PUBLISHING

Please visit our website, www.garethstevens.com. For a free color catalog of all our high-quality books, call toll free 1-800-542-2595 or fax 1-877-542-2596.

Cataloging-in-Publication Data

Names: Fletcher, Patricia.
Title: Why are ostriches so big? And other curious bird adaptations / Patricia Fletcher.
Description: New York : Gareth Stevens Publishing, 2018. | Series: Odd adaptations | Includes index.
Identifiers: ISBN 9781538203866 (pbk.) | ISBN 9781538203873 (library bound) | ISBN 9781538203675 (6 pack)
Subjects: LCSH: Ostriches–Juvenile literature. | Adaptation (Biology)–Juvenile literature.
Classification: LCC QL696.S9 F54 2018 | DDC 598.5'24–dc23

First Edition

Published in 2018 by
Gareth Stevens Publishing
111 East 14th Street, Suite 349
New York, NY 10003

Copyright © 2018 Gareth Stevens Publishing

Designer: Sarah Liddell
Editor: Kristen Nelson

Photo credits: Cover, p. 1 Coffeemill/Shutterstock.com; background used throughout Captblack76/Shutterstock.com; p. 4 rlsmithtx/Shutterstock.com; p. 5 Super Prin/Shutterstock.com; p. 6 Encyclopaedia Britannica/Contributor/Universal Images Group/Getty Images; p. 7 Soerfm/Wikimedia Commons; pp. 8, 9 Andreas Feininger/Contributor/The LIFE Picture Collection/Getty Images; p. 10 Steve Byland/Shutterstock.com; p. 11 Ondrej Prosicky/Shutterstock.com; p. 12 StockPhotoAstur/Shutterstock.com; p. 13 (snowy owl) FotoRequest/Shutterstock.com; p. 13 (duck) Richard Sharp/Shutterstock.com; p. 13 (hawk) SUSAN LEGGETT/Shutterstock.com; p. 14 (barn swallow) Dennis Jacobsen/Shutterstock.com; p. 14 (turkey) photomaster/Shutterstock.com; p. 15 Delmas Lehman/Shutterstock.com; pp. 16, 21 (sparrow) Eric Isselee/Shutterstock.com; p. 17 Ivanov Gleb/Shutterstock.com; p. 18 John Kasawa/Shutterstock.com; p. 19 Bukhanovskyy/Shutterstock.com; p. 20 Arterra/Contributor/Universal Images Group/Getty Images; p. 21 (warbler) Imfoto/Shutterstock.com; p. 21 (hawk) Lori Labrecque/Shutterstock.com; p. 21 (hummingbird) Mike Truchon/Shutterstock.com; p. 21 (pelican) Shams Ashraf/Shutterstock.com; p. 21 (heron) Brian Lasenby/Shutterstock.com; p. 22 picturepartners/Shutterstock.com; p. 23 Stubblefield Photography/Shutterstock.com; p. 24 HGalina/Shutterstock.com; p. 25 BlueRingMedia/Shutterstock.com; p. 26 milka-kotka/Shutterstock.com; p. 27 (eagle nest) Paul Reeves Photography/Shutterstock.com; p. 27 (baby cuckoo) tonchonlathorn/Shutterstock.com; p. 28 Neo Tribbiani/Shutterstock.com; p. 29 Marc van Vuren/Shutterstock.com.

Printed in China

CPSIA compliance information: Batch #CS17GS: For further information contact Gareth Stevens, New York, New York at 1-800-542-2595.

CONTENTS

Words in the glossary appear in **bold** type the first time they are used in the text.

WHAT MAKES A BIRD A BIRD?

You can tell birds from other animals because they're the only animals on Earth with feathers! In addition, all birds are warm-blooded, which means their body stays a certain temperature no matter what it's like around them. They're also all vertebrates, or have a backbone. Of course, all birds have wings and lay eggs!

Though there are many similarities among birds, there are more than 10,000 different species, or kinds, of birds. They all have adaptations that have made them better fit where they live, what they eat, and how they move—and some are pretty weird to learn about!

SOME STRANGE ADAPTATIONS ARE FOUND AMONG BIRDS AS A WHOLE GROUP. OTHERS ONLY SHOW UP IN A FEW KINDS OR EVEN JUST ONE TYPE OF BIRD!

CHANGE OVER TIME

Adaptations are the ways a species' body or behavior changes over time to make it better suited to its **environment**. Animals with favorable features or behaviors are more likely to survive, so they pass on these features. It takes a long time for an adaptation to spread among a species.

5

BIRD OR DINOSAUR?

Around 1860, scientists first discovered fossils of *Archaeopteryx*. This animal lived about 150 million years ago—it's one of the oldest known birds!

Archaeopteryx had more in common with dinosaurs than with modern birds. It had teeth and a long, bony tail. It also had feathers and a body structure that tells scientists it could fly—though not very well or for long distances.

Another ancient bird fossil, *Xiaotingia zhengi*, was found in China and announced in 2011. Though both *Archaeopteryx* and *X. zhengi* share a lot of features with dinosaurs, scientists commonly put them in the group Avialae—the group that includes all birds, both living and extinct.

ARCHAEOPTERYX SKELETON

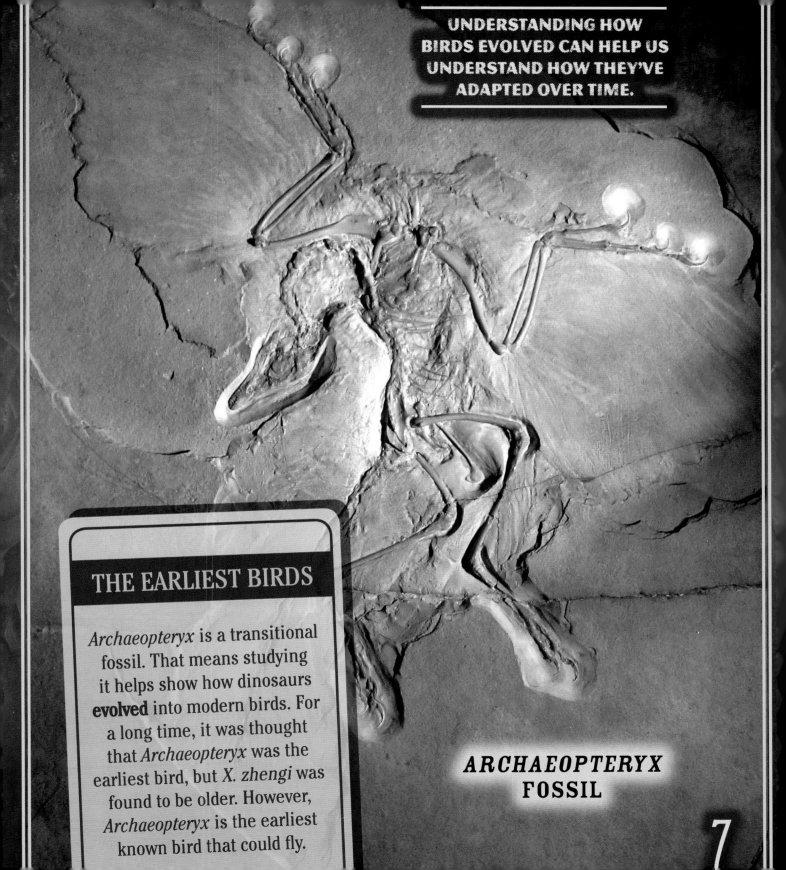

THE EARLIEST BIRDS

Archaeopteryx is a transitional fossil. That means studying it helps show how dinosaurs **evolved** into modern birds. For a long time, it was thought that *Archaeopteryx* was the earliest bird, but *X. zhengi* was found to be older. However, *Archaeopteryx* is the earliest known bird that could fly.

ARCHAEOPTERYX FOSSIL

THE ODD BIRD BODY

SOME OF BIRDS' BONES ARE HOLLOW! They have air cavities, or open spaces, in them. Some of their dinosaur **ancestors** had similarly hollow bones. That means this adaptation didn't evolve just for flight. However, modern birds have many more bones with this feature, likely to help with flight. In fact, the larger a bird is and the more flying it does, the more air cavities its bones have!

The air cavities don't mean birds' skeletons are lightweight—they're just as heavy as those of other animals their size! Birds have **dense** bones that are strong and stiff, making their body able to handle taking off and landing!

BONES WITH AIR CAVITIES IN THEM ARE CALLED PNEUMATIC (NYOO-MAA-TIHK) BONES.

PNEUMATIC BONE

BETTER BONES FOR FLIGHT

Other skeletal adaptations occurred in birds to make them better fliers. They grew fewer bones over time, and some bones fused. Some of the hollow bones have tiny struts inside them. Struts are little bars that support the walls of the birds' bones against the pressures of flight and other activities.

BIRDS HAVE A LARGER AND MORE EFFICIENT RESPIRATORY, OR BREATHING, SYSTEM THAN PEOPLE! They have small lungs plus about nine air sacs used to pump air in and out of the body. Sometimes, these air sacs are found in a bird's bones. That means birds' hollow bones are important for breathing as well as flight!

A bird heart has four main parts, like the human heart. It pumps out oxygen-rich blood to the body and brings back oxygen-poor blood. Unlike people, birds' respiratory system is so good, birds only need one breath for every six to 10 heartbeats. People take about one breath for about every 4 1/2 heartbeats!

WHAT A BIRD BRAIN!

Birds have a big brain and an excellent **nervous system** to help them use what they see and **respond** to it quickly. Birds are able to fly around trees and buildings and away from predators with seeming ease because the commands from the brain are passed to the rest of the body so fast.

HUMMINGBIRDS TAKE ABOUT 250 BREATHS EVERY MINUTE, WHILE PEOPLE ONLY TAKE ABOUT 12 TO 20. HUMMINGBIRDS BREATHE EVEN FASTER WHEN FLYING!

IT'S IMPORTANT FOR BIRDS TO BE ABLE TO BREATHE IN AND USE OXYGEN VERY WELL BECAUSE FLYING IS A LOT OF WORK.

11

The size, shape, and look of a bird's feet are adapted to its environment and how it lives. **THOUGH BOTH ARE BIRDS, A ROBIN'S FEET LOOK TOTALLY DIFFERENT FROM A FALCON'S!**

Woodpeckers have two toes facing forward and two facing backward. This lets them climb up, down, and even sideways on trees!

Raptors, or birds such as owls and hawks, have large claws called talons. They use their talons to catch and carry prey and even kill it!

Water birds have webbed feet. Some, like ducks, use them for swimming. Others, like gulls, need webbing so they can walk in soft sand or mud.

WOODPECKER

TOUGH OLD BIRDS

Most birds' feet have a scaly-looking skin, which makes their feet stronger. Their feet are mostly bones and **tendons** so they're able to land on cold surfaces. They don't feel the cold like you would. They can make the blood vessels in their feet smaller when it's very cold outside, too.

12

DUCK

SNOWY OWLS HAVE FEATHERS ON THEIR FEET! THEY OFTEN LIVE WHERE IT'S VERY COLD AND NEED EXTRA PROTECTION.

HAWK

13

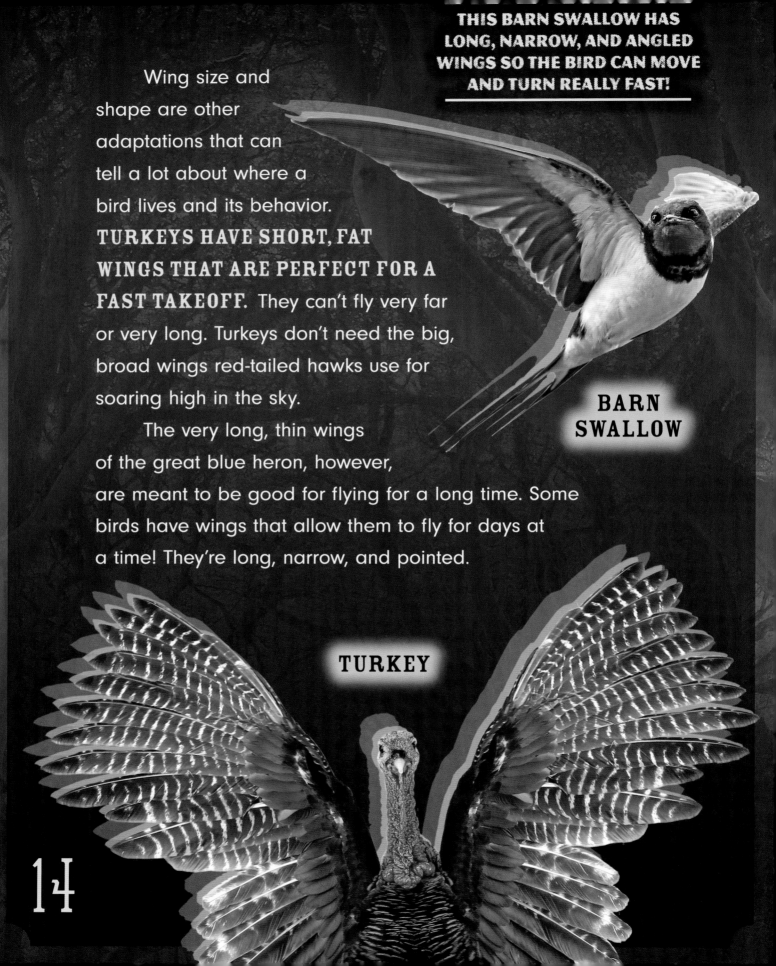

Wing size and shape are other adaptations that can tell a lot about where a bird lives and its behavior. **TURKEYS HAVE SHORT, FAT WINGS THAT ARE PERFECT FOR A FAST TAKEOFF.** They can't fly very far or very long. Turkeys don't need the big, broad wings red-tailed hawks use for soaring high in the sky.

The very long, thin wings of the great blue heron, however, are meant to be good for flying for a long time. Some birds have wings that allow them to fly for days at a time! They're long, narrow, and pointed.

BARN SWALLOW

TURKEY

14

HEADING SOUTH FOR THE WINTER

Some kinds of birds have adapted to their environment by leaving it when the weather changes! This is called migration. Birds often migrate during colder months to find food. In order to migrate long distances, birds would need to have wings adapted to flying as far as is needed!

15

THE HUGE OSTRICH

Ostriches can weigh hundreds of pounds and grow to be 9 feet (2.7 m) tall. Their eggs can weigh as much as 3 pounds (1.4 kg)! **OSTRICHES EVOLVED TO BE THE LARGEST BIRDS ON EARTH.**

How did ostriches get to be so big? It all started about 180 million years ago. The huge continent that included Australia, New Zealand, South America, Africa, and Antarctica began to break apart. Groups of a small, flying, ground-feeding bird that also ran well were split up. They wound up in places where they had lots of food. After their dinosaur predators died out, the flying birds evolved into large, flightless birds.

KIWI

HUGE, BUT GROUNDED

The large, flightless birds are called ratites. Besides ostriches, they include kiwis, rheas, emus, and a few species that have died out. When the dinosaurs died out about 65 million years ago, there weren't any more large predators. **THE RATITES' FLYING ANCESTOR COULD GIVE UP FLYING AND GROW LARGER.**

THOUGH OSTRICHES DON'T FLY, THEY'RE ABLE TO RUN AS FAST AS A CAR ON A CITY STREET!

17

FROM TEETH TO BEAKS

UNTIL ABOUT 100 MILLION YEARS AGO, BIRDS HAD TEETH. Even more bizarre, birds can *still* possibly grow teeth! Over time, the genes used to grow teeth got turned off. But they're still in bird DNA! In 2006, scientists figured out how to turn these genes on again. They made chickens grow teeth!

People once believed birds stopped growing teeth to be lighter and better fliers. However, *Archaeopteryx* had teeth and flew, so that may not be true! Scientists are working to discover why birds' teeth-growing genes turned off when crocodiles, which are closely related to birds, have kept theirs on.

CROCODILE

CAN YOU IMAGINE WHAT A CHICKEN WOULD LOOK LIKE WITH A CROCODILE'S TEETH? SCARY!

TEETH PASSED DOWN AND OUT

Birds didn't lose their teeth all at once. First, about 116 million years ago, birds stopped making enamel, one of the main kinds of matter that make up teeth. By 100 million years ago, birds were no longer making dentin, another major part of teeth. This shows that birds' tooth loss happened over the course of many generations of birds.

Birds seem to have evolved beaks around the time they lost their teeth. **IN FACT, THERE ARE FOSSILS OF BIRD ANCESTORS THAT HAVE PART OF A BEAK IN FRONT AND TEETH IN THE BACK!**

Some birds eat fish, others hunt small animals, and still others only eat nuts and seeds. They need different beaks, or bills, in order to eat how they like to. Modern bird species' beaks are specially adapted to what, where, and how each kind of bird eats!

BITE YOUR TONGUE!

A bird's tongue works with its beak to catch food and eat it. In many species, its size and shape are special adaptations, too! A bird's tongue can be long, short, and even have barbs, or little hooks, on it. **WHAT'S MORE, BIRDS HAVE TASTE BUDS.** Chickens have about 24, pigeons as many as 59, and parrots between 300 and 400.

MALLARDS, A KIND OF DUCK, HAVE LAMELLAE (LUH-*MEH*-LEE) ON THE INSIDE EDGES OF THEIR BILL. THESE ARE COMBLIKE AND HELP KEEP FOOD INSIDE THE MALLARD'S MOUTH, WHILE MUD AND WATER CAN ESCAPE.

LAMELLAE

ALL ABOUT BEAKS

BEAK TYPE	USED FOR...	BIRD EXAMPLES
CONE SHAPED	CRACKING SEEDS AND NUTS	FINCH, GROSBEAK, SPARROW
THIN, POINTED	PICKING INSECTS OFF LEAVES AND BARK	WARBLER, WREN, ORIOLE
HOOKED	BITING AND TEARING PREY	HAWK, OWL
LONG, TUBELIKE	DRINKING NECTAR	HUMMINGBIRD
POUCHES	CATCHING FISH AND HOLDING WATER	PELICAN
SPEARS	STABBING AT FISH IN THE WATER	HERON, KINGFISHER, TERN

SPARROW

WARBLER

HAWK

HUMMINGBIRD

PELICAN

HERON

RIGHT IN THE GIZZARD!

Even with a beak, birds don't chew their food. **INSTEAD, BIRDS HAVE A WEIRD BODY PART CALLED THE GIZZARD THAT HELPS THEM DO IT!**

Once a bird's food is swallowed, it moves into a tube called the esophagus. Many kinds of birds store food in a part called the crop. There, it gets softer before moving on to the first part of the bird's stomach, called the proventriculus. Food starts to break down there.

Food then moves to the second part of the stomach, the gizzard. **THERE MAY BE SAND OR SMALL ROCKS IN A BIRD'S GIZZARD THAT HELP GRIND UP THE FOOD!**

OWL PELLET

22

GROSS GIZZARD

The gizzard is a muscle. The sand, stones, and other "grit" in it are swallowed along with a bird's food. Birds that swallow food whole, such as owls, have bones and feathers in their gizzard! Their body takes all the water from these parts, and they cough up the rest as tiny hard matter called a pellet.

FOOD GETS GROUND UP IN THE GIZZARD SO BIRDS CAN TAKE IN THE **NUTRIENTS** FOUND IN IT. BIRDS THAT EAT HARDER FOODS, SUCH AS NUTS AND SEEDS, HAVE THICKER, STRONGER GIZZARDS.

23

WASTE MANAGEMENT

CHICKENS DON'T PEE! Actually, no birds do. All their waste is the soft, whitish stuff you might find on a car windshield! It's not quite a liquid, but not quite a solid, either.

Once birds digest, or break down, their food, solid waste moves through their large intestine to a **chamber** called the cloaca (kloh-AY-kuh). There, it's joined by liquid waste their kidneys have removed from their blood. Birds can remove water from the waste in the cloaca. **THIS ADAPTATION ALLOWS THEM TO PRESERVE WATER, MAKING IT POSSIBLE FOR THEM TO GO LONGER BETWEEN DRINKING.** They also don't have to take pit stops when flying!

SALTY SEABIRDS

In order to take in enough water, seabirds have adapted to drinking salt water. The salt they take in travels through their blood to a pair of **glands** over their eyes. The salty liquid runs out of and down their beak, falling back into the water!

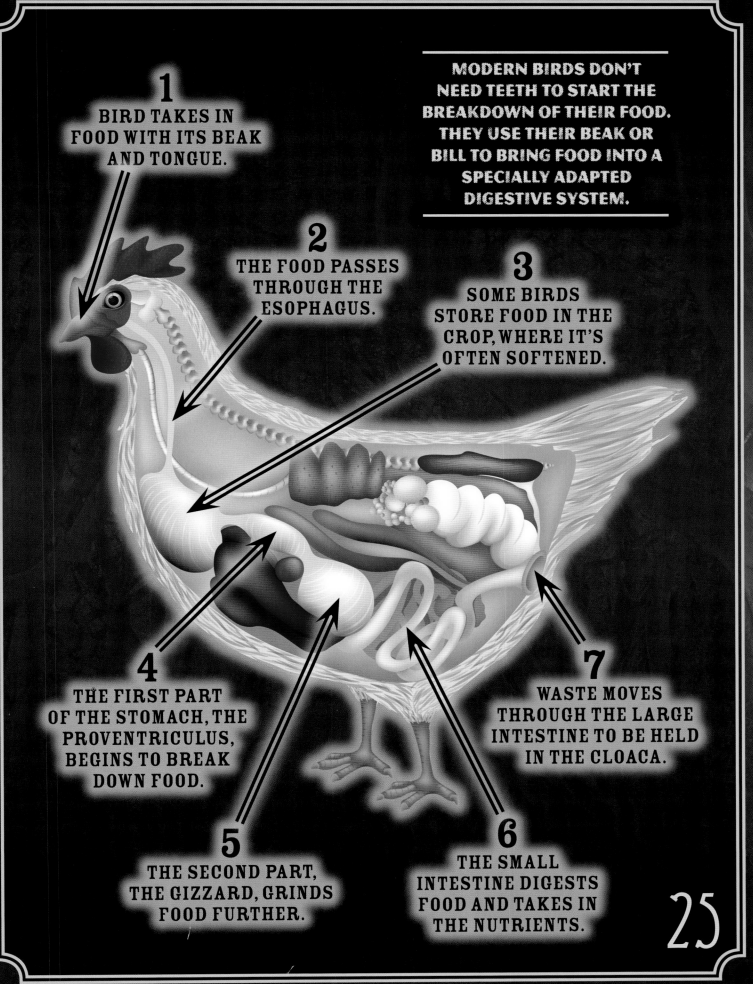

SUPER SHELLS

Birds' eggs have a hard shell that protects the baby inside. The size and color of these eggs depend on the kind of bird! These adaptations help the birds inside the eggs have a better chance of surviving.

The least tern has light brown eggs with darker spots, which blend in to the sandy environment they're laid in. **A BIRD'S EGGS NEED TO BLEND IN BECAUSE PARENT BIRDS CAN'T ALWAYS BE SITTING ON THEM.**

Birds' eggs are shaped for protection, too. Birds that build nests in high places have eggs that are smaller on one end. This makes the eggs more likely to roll in a circle—instead of off a cliff!

LEAST TERN EGGS

HOW A BIRD BUILDS ITS NEST IS AN ADAPTATION, TOO. THIS EAGLE'S NEST IS CALLED AN AERIE (*EHR-EE*). EAGLES USE THE SAME AERIE EVERY YEAR!

BABY CUCKOO

THE SNEAKY CUCKOO

LIKE OTHER BIRDS, CUCKOOS LAY EGGS—BUT THEY LAY THEM IN OTHER BIRDS' NESTS! They let other mother birds, such as magpies and starlings, sit on their eggs until they hatch. Then, the baby cuckoo pushes other chicks out of the nest so it can get more food! What an odd adaptation!

27

BIRDIE TALK

Tweet tweet! Caw caw! Chirp! Birds make lots of different sounds. Do you ever wonder why? Birds sing, call, squeak, click, and make lots of other sounds to ask for food, tell their chicks where they are, or tell other birds to keep away. **THE RUFFED GROUSE TELLS OTHER BIRDS WHERE ITS TERRITORY IS BY FLAPPING ITS WINGS IN SUCH A WAY THAT IT CREATES A LITTLE SONIC BOOM!**

Birds talk to each other through how they move and show their feathers, too. This is called a display. Displays are often used when birds are looking for a mate!

PARROT

THEY SAY THE DARNDEST THINGS!

Some pet birds, such as parrots, are trained to talk to their owners. While it would be a truly weird adaptation if birds could talk, these birds are simply able to copy sounds, including human language. African grey parrots are one kind good at learning words and phrases.

MALE PEACOCKS OPEN THEIR BEAUTIFUL TAIL TO DRAW IN FEMALES. THEY ALSO SHAKE THEIR TAIL AT OTHER BIRDS TO TELL THEM TO GET AWAY!

29

GLOSSARY

ancestor: an animal that lived before others in its family tree

chamber: a space used for a certain purpose

dense: packed very closely together

efficient: having to do with the most effective or purposeful way of doing something

environment: the conditions that surround a living thing and affect the way it lives

evolve: to grow and change over time

gland: a body part that produces something needed for a bodily function

nervous system: the body system made up of the brain, spine, and nerves

nutrient: something a living thing needs to grow and stay alive

respond: to act after something happens

sonic boom: the sound made when something moves faster than the speed of sound

tendon: a band of tough tissue that connects muscles and bones

FOR MORE INFORMATION

BOOKS

Earley, Chris. *Weird Birds*. Buffalo, NY: Firefly Books, 2014.

Gray, Susan H. *The Life Cycle of Birds*. Chicago, IL: Heinemann Library, 2012.

WEBSITES

Birds
kids.nationalgeographic.com/animals/hubs/birds/
Read about many kinds of birds—and their cool adaptations!

Ostrich
animals.sandiegozoo.org/animals/ostrich
Find out more about the largest bird on Earth.

Parrot Life Cycle Game
www.sheppardsoftware.com/scienceforkids/life_cycle/bird_lifecycle.htm
Play a game to learn more about birds' life cycle.

INDEX